CONTEMPORARY LIVES

MILEY CYRUS

POP PRINCESS

CONTEMPORARY LIVES

MILEY CYRUS

POP PRINCESS
by Jennifer Joline Anderson

Essential Library

An Imprint of Abdo Publishing | www.abdopublishing.com

www.abdopublishing.com

Published by Abdo Publishing, a division of ABDO, PO Box 398166, Minneapolis, Minnesota 55439. Copyright © 2015 by Abdo Consulting Group, Inc. International copyrights reserved in all countries. No part of this book may be reproduced in any form without written permission from the publisher. Essential Library™ is a trademark and logo of Abdo Publishing.

Printed in the United States of America, North Mankato, Minnesota
102014
012015

THIS BOOK CONTAINS
RECYCLED MATERIALS

Cover Photo: Helga Esteb/Shutterstock Images
Interior Photos: Helga Esteb/Shutterstock Images, 3; Charles Sykes/Invision/AP Images, 6–7, 90, 98; Evan Agostini/Invision/AP Images, 10; Jaguar PS/Shutterstock Images, 14; MS2 Wenn Photos/Newscom, 16–17; Eric Charbonneau/Invision/AP Images, 22, 66–67; Solo/Zuma Press/Newscom, 24; The Disney Channel/Photofest, 25–26, 42–43, 45, 97 (top); Seth Poppel/Yearbook Library, 30; Jean-Pierre Muller/AFP/Getty Images/Newscom, 33; KH1 Wenn Photos/Newscom, 34–35; William Scott/AdMedia/Newscom, 40; GM1 Wenn Photos/Newscom, 51; Jeff Christensen/AP Images, 52–53, 96; Chris Pizzello/AP Images, 56; Everett Collection/Shutterstock Images, 58–59, 61; s_bukley/Shutterstock Images, 65, 69, 81, 97 (bottom); Walt Disney Pictures/Photofest, 72; Jordan Strauss/Invision/AP Images, 74–75; ABC/Photofest, 76, 99 (top); Matt Sayles/AP Images, 82; Giulio Marcocchi/Sipa USA/AP Images, 84–85, 100; David Silpa/UPI/Newscom, 87; Kevin Mazur/MTV1415/WireImage/Getty Images, 95, 99 (bottom)

Editor: Megan Anderson
Series Designer: Emily Love

Library of Congress Control Number: 2014943855

Cataloging-in-Publication Data

Anderson, Jennifer Joline.
 Miley Cyrus: pop princess / Jennifer Joline Anderson.
 p. cm. -- (Contemporary lives)
Includes bibliographical references and index.
ISBN 978-1-62403-544-9
1. Cyrus, Miley, 1992- --Juvenile literature. 2. Singers--United States--Biography--Juvenile literature. 3. Television actors and actresses--United States--Biography--Juvenile literature. 1. Title.
782.42164092--dc23
[B]

2014943855

CONTENTS

Reaction to Cyrus's risqué
performance at the
2013 MTV Video Music Awards
took over social media.

CHAPTER 1

A Shocking Performance

|||||||||||||||||||||||||||||||||||||||||||||||||||||||||||||||||||||||

On August 25, 2013, 10.1 million viewers tuned into the 2013 MTV Video Music Awards (VMAs), broadcast live from Brooklyn, New York.[1] A star-studded audience packed the Barclays Center. Among the nominees set to perform were Lady Gaga, Justin Timberlake, Bruno Mars, and Taylor Swift. But they were all about to be upstaged by Miley Cyrus.

The VMAs are awards presented by cable channel MTV to honor the year's best music videos. The awards ceremony has been broadcast live on MTV every year since 1984. The award is a statuette in the form of an astronaut on the moon, dubbed the "Moon Man."

Cyrus was no stranger to the spotlight. The daughter of country singer Billy Ray Cyrus, she had been in the public eye since birth. At age two, she toddled onstage at her father's performances to meet music legends such as Aretha Franklin and Tony Bennett. Cyrus had been a megastar in her own right since age 12, when she burst onto the scene playing a teen pop star on Disney's hit television series *Hannah Montana*. That show, along with its soundtrack albums, sold-out concert tours, and assorted merchandise, made Cyrus into a multimillionaire. At the time, she was the richest teenager in Hollywood.

But by 2013, Cyrus was 20 years old—not a teenager anymore. Since *Hannah Montana* had gone off the air two years before, she had been trying to prove she was more than just a sugary-sweet pop singer on the Disney Channel. She was ready to change her image in a dramatic way. In place of her long brown hair and flowing blonde wigs, she now had a punk-style buzz cut. Her 2013 album, *Bangerz*, had a hip-hop sound far removed from her country music roots.

Now she was looking forward to the VMAs as her chance to show off the new Miley Cyrus. In fact, she promised her fans, she was about to pull a stunt that would top anything done at the awards show before. It would be, she announced, the "best VMA performance of all time."[2]

‖‖

"A TRAIN WRECK"

Arriving at the VMAs, Cyrus leapt onto the red carpet in a skin-tight black outfit decorated with bold, colorful jewels. Her short blonde hair was twisted into two small buns that looked like horns. She stuck out her tongue at photographers, a move she had become known for in recent months. The cameras followed her backstage, where she jumped up and down in excitement and nervousness as she prepared for her big moment.

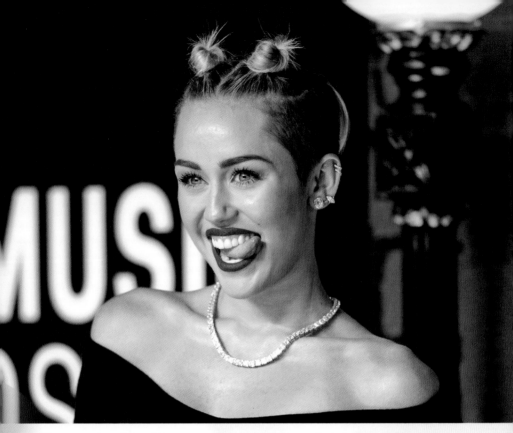

The opposite of her Disney star look, Cyrus's new hairstyle and behavior was an attempt to shake up her image.

Cyrus was set to perform her hit single "We Can't Stop," which was nominated for several awards. The stage set looked like something out of a bizarre dream. Dancers dressed as pink teddy bears lined up facing the audience. A giant robot bear towered over them, lights flashing across its visor. The stage was bathed in electric blue light and searchlights swept the crowd as eerie, synthesized percussion boomed ominously.

Suddenly, a trapdoor in the robot bear's body swung open to reveal Cyrus, wearing a silver leotard with the face of a winking bear on the front.

Cyrus strutted onto the stage and launched into an awkward, jerky dance alongside the pink bears, kicking her legs and wagging her tongue. "Let's make some noise!" she shouted.[3] The pink bears swayed to the music, waving at the audience. As she performed her song, three backup dancers joined Cyrus with teddy bears strapped to their backs. Together they performed a hip-thrusting, bottom-shaking dance move called "twerking." Cyrus even bent over and shook her bottom at the audience before belting out the song's chorus, "It's our party, we can do what we want to!"[4]

Next, Cyrus and singer Robin Thicke performed a duet of his song "Blurred Lines." As Thicke

"I HATE SMILING IN PICTURES" ||||||||||||||||||||||||||||||||||||

In an interview with *Rolling Stone* magazine, Miley explained why she is so often pictured sticking out her tongue, a pose she admitted her mother hates. "I just stick my tongue out because I hate smiling in pictures," she said. "Every other girl is so serious—like, 'This is my moment on the red carpet, I'm in my ball gown, looking pretty.' There's something empowering about what I'm doing right now."[5]

stepped onstage in a black-and-white striped suit, Cyrus ripped off her teddy bear costume to reveal a flesh-colored bikini that made her appear nude. She danced around Thicke, rubbing against him and jabbing him with a foam finger in a lewd, vulgar way.

As Cyrus performed, the cameras swept the crowd, capturing embarrassed laughter and stares of disbelief. While many audience members roared with approval at the onstage spectacle, others seemed to wonder if it was a joke. Meanwhile, the

A CONTROVERSIAL DANCE MOVE ||||||||||||||||||||||||||||||||

Twerking is a style of dance that emerged in the New Orleans hip-hop scene in the 1990s. The dance move is particularly rooted in African American culture. Because the dance involves jerking the hips in a sexual way, it is often criticized as vulgar and raunchy. Cyrus created a twerking trend in 2013 when she posted a goofy YouTube video of herself twerking to the song "Wop" by rapper J. Dash while wearing a unicorn costume. But many also thought Cyrus's twerking, as well as her VMA performance as a whole, was cultural appropriation. Critics accused her of using parts of black culture to rework her image. Jody Rosen of *Vulture* said Cyrus adopted certain elements of black culture and "the potent sexual symbolism of black female bodies, to the cause of her reinvention . . . Her act tipped over into what we may as well just call racism."[6]

immediate reaction in the press was one of shock and disgust. One reporter called the performance "a train wreck" that had caused "confusion, dismay and horror."[7] The Parents Television Council blasted MTV for airing a show inappropriate for a family audience. Hundreds of parents agreed, voicing their concern that the former Disney star was setting a terrible example for her young fans. "Miley wrongly represents the way girls should act today," one grandparent said in a CNN article.[8]

||||||||||||||||||||||||||||||||||||||||||||||||||||||||||||

THE LAST LAUGH

As the negative comments swirled around on television and the Internet, Cyrus only laughed. She said her performance was meant to be funny and people were taking it way too seriously. "I don't pay attention to the negative," she claimed. "You're always going to make people talk; you might as well make them talk for, like, two weeks rather than two seconds."[9]

And talk they did. In the hours after her shocking VMA performance, Cyrus was mentioned 300,000 times per minute on Twitter. She added 100,000 followers to her Instagram account and

MEMORABLE VMA MOMENTS

Cyrus's performance at the 2013 MTV Video Music Awards was hardly the first shocking act seen on the program. In 1984, the first year the awards show aired, Madonna raised eyebrows by performing her hit "Like a Virgin" in a sexy wedding gown. In 2003, Madonna and Britney Spears created a stir by kissing onstage. And in 2009, Lady Gaga horrified the audience with a costume that made it appear as though she were bleeding. As Cyrus described the awards show: "It's meant to be fun. It's meant to push the boundaries."[11]

50,000 likes on Facebook.[10] Amid all the chatter, her new song "Wrecking Ball" rocketed to the Number 2 spot on the iTunes charts.

For all the negative press, Miley Cyrus got the last laugh. She did not win a single award in any of her nominated categories. But whether people loved her performance or hated it, whether they got the joke or not, Cyrus definitely was the winner. For the next few weeks, she was the most talked-about performer in the country.

Billy Ray has always supported his daughter's ascent to stardom.

MGM GRAND

ACA
of COU

Miley grew up in a
music-loving household.

CHAPTER 2

Daughter of a Country Star

||||||||||||||||||||||||||||||||||||||||||||||||||||||||||||||||||||||||||||||||||||

Destiny Hope Cyrus was born on November 23, 1992, in Nashville, Tennessee, to country singer Billy Ray Cyrus and Leticia "Tish" Finley, a former model. At the time of his daughter's birth, Billy Ray was riding high on the fame of his hit song "Achy Breaky Heart." He was sure his tiny daughter had a special future, so he gave her the name Destiny Hope. But he soon nicknamed the happy baby

"Smiley Miley." That was shortened to Miley, and the name stuck.

|||||||||||||||||||||||||||||||||||||||||||||||||||||

DADDY'S GIRL

Miley's father, Billy Ray, was born into a musical family in Flatwoods, Kentucky. His parents both loved to play and sing. He dropped out of school and started a band called Sly Dog with his brother and a few friends. After that, Billy Ray spent several years knocking on doors in the country music capital of Nashville, as well as Los Angeles, California, hoping to land a recording contract.

A MUSICAL FAMILY |||||||||||||||||||||||||||||||||||||||||||||||||||||||||||

Miley grew up in a musical family. Her great-grandfather E. L. Cyrus was a preacher in the Pentecostal Church. Gospel music was a part of the worship service. Her grandfather Ronald Ray Cyrus sang in a gospel group called the Crownsmen Quartet. He went on to become a successful politician in his home state of Kentucky. Grandmother Ruthie Cyrus played the piano, and both Billy Ray and his brother Kebo played guitar. At family gatherings, Miley remembered, the house would fill with music. Miley's brother Trace is also a musician, best known for founding the indie rock band Metro Station, and sister Brandi plays guitar and sings.

Billy Ray's big break came in 1990 when he was signed with a major label, Mercury Records. When his first album, *Some Gave All,* was released in 1992, it was the Number 1 record in the US for seventeen weeks and sold 20 million copies. The big hit on the record was the catchy dance tune "Achy Breaky Heart." It topped the country music charts and became a crossover hit on pop radio stations, peaking at Number 4 on the *Billboard* Hot 100. Female fans swooned over Billy Ray's good looks and men copied his trademark hairstyle, the mullet. Seemingly overnight, Billy Ray became a world-famous singer and a multimillionaire.

In addition to success, Billy Ray also found love. His future wife, Tish, appeared in his video for "Achy Breaky Heart." Soon he became a new father. The proud parent loved having his daughter along on tour. Miley was eager to share the spotlight with him, saying,

> *I sat on his shoulders in front of thousands of people. . . . Sometimes he'd bring me onstage to sing "Hound Dog" with him, and I'm told they had some trouble getting me off. At the end of each show, when the fans gave him gifts, I'd run*

*out in front of the cheering crowd, help my daddy
gather [them] up.*[1]

Growing up as her father's little shadow, it was
no surprise Miley learned to love music. "Dad
always says that I could sing before I could talk,"[2]
she said. "If I was onstage singing, she would break
free from her nanny or her mom, run on stage,
and grab the nearest microphone," her father said.[3]
Miley was definitely her daddy's girl.

|||||||||||||||||||||||||||||||||||||||||||||||||||||||||||

A COUNTRY CHILDHOOD

Although the pressures of celebrity made it
difficult, Billy Ray was determined to be a good
father and family man. Miley's parents married
a year after she was born. Soon after, the family
moved to a large farm outside of Franklin,
Tennessee, a suburb of Nashville. The farm was
a peaceful place offering an escape from tabloid
reporters and paparazzi, where Miley could have a
normal childhood.

The Cyrus clan was a blended family. When
Miley's parents met, Tish already had two
children—Brandi, born in 1987, and Trace, born

MILEY'S PETS

Miley had many pets growing up on the family farm, including Eeyore the donkey, Lucy the chicken, and goldfish named Lyric and Melody. Her favorite pets have always been her dogs. Today, she has five canine pals: Emu, Bean, Penny Lane, Mary Jane, and Happy. All five are rescue animals.

in 1989. Billy Ray adopted them after he and Tish were married, so Miley grew up with an older sister and brother. A younger brother, Braison, was born in 1994, and baby sister Noah came along in 2000. Miley also had a fifth sibling, Christopher Cody, the son of Billy Ray and a previous girlfriend. Christopher was just eight months older than Miley, but grew up with his mother in Texas, and Miley rarely saw him.

Miley grew up a country girl. She and her siblings went barefoot outdoors and rode horses and four-wheelers. Besides horses, the farm had chickens, cows, dogs, cats, and even a donkey named Eeyore. "Our house is a loud, busy place with family and friends and animals coming and going," she wrote in her autobiography.[4]

From left: Billy Ray, Miley, Braison, Noah, Trace, Brandi, and Tish Cyrus.

Billy Ray was frequently on the road for concert tours, but when he was home, Miley and her father were inseparable.

> *We'd go four-wheeling or dirt biking all day, ending up at the top of a hill where there's a tipi to camp in. . . . We'd sit there next to that fire, with the trees and the big Tennessee sky. It was easy to start dreaming big under all those stars. . . . I spent most of my childhood outside with my dad.[5]*

Living in the country, Miley's siblings were her best friends. In her autobiography, she recalls spending hours bouncing on a trampoline with her sister Brandi, putting makeup on little sister Noah, and building a tree house with her brothers Trace and Braison, whom she nicknamed "Trazz" and "Brazz."

Miley was also close with her grandparents. Her grandfather Ronald Ray Cyrus, whom she called "Pappy," would take her fishing. He loved to tease. When he bought Miley a pet donkey, he had her convinced the animal was part zebra. Miley also adored her grandma, or "Mammie," Loretta Finley, who was like a second mother to her.

Later, when Miley became a celebrity, she credited her close family with keeping her down to earth. "My family makes it pretty darn easy to stay grounded and remember where I come from and who I really am," she said.[6]

||||||||||||||||||||||||||||||||||||||||||||||||||||||||||||||

LIFE WITH A FAMOUS DAD

Although in some ways Miley had an ordinary country childhood, in other ways it was far from typical. She was, after all, the daughter of a wealthy celebrity. The Cyrus home was no humble farm,

Country music legend Dolly Parton is Miley's godmother.

but a huge estate that sprawled over 500 acres (200 ha), and the house was a mansion with an indoor pool.

Miley also grew up around famous people, including her godmother, country music superstar Dolly Parton, whom she calls "Aunt Dolly." Miley was never shy around her father's musician friends. Her outgoing personality led to unforgettable encounters as well as opportunities for her to learn more about making music. Ed King, the guitarist for the southern rock band Lynyrd Skynyrd, showed Miley how to play "Sweet Home Alabama" on her first guitar. When country legend Waylon Jennings visited the house, Miley brought out her guitar and asked him for a lesson. She put her face close to the guitar while he played a song, watching closely to see how he formed the chords. "I was amazed at Miley's curiosity and fearlessness," her father recalled. "She was like a sponge."[7]

"Having a famous dad was kind of cool," Miley said. "That's where I got the idea that I wanted to sing and act. . . . If it wasn't for my dad, I never would have discovered that I love it."[8]

|||||||||||

AUNT DOLLY

Miley's godmother, Dolly Parton, is a country music legend with 25 Number 1 songs and many awards over her long career. She has written more than 3,000 songs, including "I Will Always Love You," which became a hit for singer Whitney Houston. Miley frequently sings her godmother's song "Jolene" in concert. "I don't think people really realize yet what a great singer and writer she really is," Parton said of Miley in November 2013. "I've loved her through the years and watched her grow up, and I've seen how smart she is and how talented she is. . . . She's just trying to find her own place and wings and learn to fly."[9]

Miley's first guitar was a Daisy Rock, a lighter-weight guitar meant for children.

CHAPTER 3

"This Is What I Want to Do"

||||||||||||||||||||||||||||||||||||||||||||||||||||||||||||||||||||||||||||||||||||||||||||

From a young age, Miley lived to perform. As the middle child in a big family, she learned singing and dancing were a way to get noticed. As she described it in her autobiography:

> I'm a middle child, with kids older than me and kids younger than me. The older ones are responsible. The younger ones are adorable. Me, I'm

A YOUNG SONGWRITER

In the 2013 MTV documentary *Miley: The Movement*, Miley recalled getting her first guitar at age eight. At first, she didn't know how to hold the guitar; she held it upside-down in imitation of her father, who is left-handed. At age 12 she began taking formal lessons. She loved writing songs and recording them with her dad on a cassette player, then listening to the cassettes in her dad's truck. "That's when I first really started loving music," she said.[2]

in the middle, singing and dancing and generally making a big show of one kind or another in an endless effort to get attention. . . . No matter how famous or successful I am, I'll always be an attention-craving middle child at heart.[1]

Miley frequently recruited her siblings to be part of the act, especially brother Braison, who was two years younger. They would sing and dance in front of a mirror or video camera, or put on a show for anyone who happened to visit. She also loved to ham it up at Heritage Elementary School. She acted in school plays, sang in choir, and was on the dance team. Outside of school, she was a competitive cheerleader who won trophies for challenging gymnastics routines. Soon, she had her chance to perform for a much larger audience.

||||||||||||||||||||||||||||||||||||||||||||||||||||||||

BITTEN BY THE ACTING BUG

In 2000, when Miley was eight years old, Billy Ray was offered the starring role in a new television series, *Doc*. The show was about a country doctor who had moved to New York, bringing his hometown values to the big city. It was a good fit for Billy Ray, who had become frustrated with the

CHEERLEADING ||||||||||||||||||||||||||||||||||||||||||||||||||||||||||||||||||||||||||||||||||

Miley was a competitive cheerleader from the age of six. Being small and petite, she was a natural for the lifts and other acrobatic feats needed in the sport. Cheerleading taught her discipline and hard work, traits that would be important later in her career. "I was at the gym every day," she recalled. "I was really into it."[3] Her competitive spirit was fierce. Once, she insisted on competing while sick with the flu, even though her coach tried to stop her. "I went out, did the routine, walked off the stage and threw up . . . But I did it. And that was what mattered to me."[4]

The pressure of cheerleading also prepared her for the auditions she would go through later when she searched for acting roles. She learned to be tough and confident and not let herself be crushed by failure or rejection.

Miley as a third grader at Heritage Elementary School

music business. Since the craze over "Achy Breaky Heart" fizzled out, his popularity had faded, too. None of his newer albums could match the success of his debut, and critics branded him a one-hit wonder. Billy Ray welcomed the career change as a way to start fresh.

Doc aired on the PAX network from March 11, 2001, through November 28, 2004. The show was filmed in Toronto, Canada, a long way from

Nashville, and Billy Ray had to be away from home much of the time. The separation was hard on the family, and they flew back and forth from Nashville to Toronto as often as they could. Miley spent a lot of time hanging around the set of *Doc*. The producers offered her a small part on the show as a young girl named Kiley. She and her sister Noah appeared in three episodes.

Miley had always wanted to perform. But before *Doc*, she had been focused on singing, dancing, and playing guitar. Now she knew she liked acting too. "Playing Kiley definitely gave me the acting bug," she recalls.[5] When Billy Ray took her to see a production of the musical *Mamma Mia!*, Miley could not contain her excitement. She grabbed her

A MATTER OF FAITH

The television show *Doc* was a good fit for Billy Ray because it communicated strong Christian values, something he and Tish tried to instill in their children. As the grandson of a Pentecostal preacher, Billy Ray had always been a man of faith. The family attended church regularly and studied the Bible. Miley was baptized as a Southern Baptist before moving to Hollywood. When she first became famous, Miley credited her faith for getting her through hard times and helping her stay humble.

father's arm and said, "This is what I want to do, Daddy. I want to be an actress!"[6]

In the summer of 2002, the Cyrus clan packed their bags and moved to Toronto. Miley spent her fifth-grade year in Canada, being homeschooled by her mother, Tish. She began taking acting and singing lessons at the Armstrong Acting Studio in Toronto. With her mother's help, Miley found an agent and began auditioning for acting roles. The smiling ten-year-old appeared in a Banquet Foods commercial as a girl eating dinner with her family.

||||||||||||||||||||||||||||||||||||||||||||||||||||||

LANDING A *BIG FISH*

In early 2003, soon after filming the television commercial, Miley was picked to play a small role in the movie *Big Fish*, directed by Tim Burton. It was a big-budget film with big-name stars including Jessica Lange, Helena Bonham-Carter, and Ewan McGregor. The movie was set in Alabama, just south of her home state of Tennessee, so Miley's southern accent was perfect for the role.

Miley appeared in only one scene, playing a girl named Ruthie who tags along with a group of boys

Tim Burton directed Miley in her first film role, a 90-second scene in the movie *Big Fish*.

to spy on a witch's house. Filming wasn't exactly comfortable, as the scene took place in a swamp.

Despite the lack of glamour, Miley was thrilled to be in a movie. When the film came out in December 2003, she and her family watched it in the theater. They stood up and cheered when she appeared on the screen. Miley couldn't wait for more.

IIIIIIIIIII

Young Miley experienced rejection before she received her big break.

CHAPTER 4

Tough Enough to Make It

||||||||||||||||||||||||||||||||||||||||||||||||||||||||||||||

With the help and encouragement of her mother, Miley continued auditioning for roles in commercials and television shows. Auditioning was difficult. She had to endure the pain of rejection many times.

But Miley tried to keep a positive attitude. "My sister Brandi always told me, 'Positive minds do positive things,'" she explained. "I didn't think of it as failure. I thought of it as part of the route to success."[1]

Knowing firsthand how brutal the entertainment business could be, Billy Ray tried to discourage his daughter from pursuing her acting dream. He encouraged her to stay in school, keep with her cheerleading, and have a normal childhood. But over time, he saw she was tough enough to make it. "She just kept keeping on and never gave up hope," Billy Ray recalled.[2]

Besides the stress of auditions, Miley had another big challenge: sixth grade. After being homeschooled in Toronto for a year, she came back to Heritage Elementary School in Nashville. Several girls she thought were her friends began bullying her. They sent mean notes, stole her books, and made fun of her clothes and hair. One day the girls locked her in a bathroom for an hour. "I'll never forget how it felt to be that girl," she said.[3]

Miley had no idea why she was being bullied. She was used to being teased about her famous dad, but this was much worse. The bullying finally stopped after Miley got a note threatening physical harm and her parents told the principal.

She said of the experience: "[It] reminds me to be compassionate. To not hold grudges. To be supportive. To be there for others when I know I'm needed."[4]

||||||||||||||||||||||||||||||||||||||||||||||||||||||||||||

DISNEY CALLING

Miley dreamed of a way out of her sixth-grade misery. Then, in 2003, her agent got her an audition for a new Disney Channel series originally titled *The Secret Life of Zoe Stewart*. The show's title was eventually changed to *Hannah Montana*. It was about a schoolgirl named Zoe Stewart leading a secret double life as a pop star named Hannah

Montana. It was Miley's dream role—if she got this part, she would be able to sing and act.

But the producers weren't thinking of Miley for the lead role. Instead, they asked her to audition for the part of Lilly, the main character's best friend. Miley sent in an audition tape. A few days later, she got a call from Disney. They wanted to consider her for the lead role after all.

But after she sent in a second audition tape, she was rejected. The producers said she was too young and too small. Zoe Stewart, alias Hannah Montana, was supposed to be 15 years old, while Miley was only 11.

||||||||||||||||||||||||||||||||||||||||||||||||||

GETTING THE PART

After the initial rejection, producers kept coming back to Miley, sensing she had something special. Miley flew out to California several times to audition in person. She tried to look older by dressing in her mother's clothes and makeup, but they still rejected her for being too young and inexperienced.

On one visit, producers asked her to sing. "You can bring the whole building," Miley said brashly. "I'll sing for everybody."[6] Recalled one of the producers, "This little girl opened up her mouth and this amazing voice came out of her that was from somebody twice as big and several years older."[7] That voice convinced them Miley really could play the role of a teenage rock star. In 2004, Miley, now age 12, landed the part.

||||||||||||||||||||||||||||||||||||||||||||||||||||||||

WORKING WITH DAD

Miley's new role meant huge changes. She would have to move to Los Angeles, and have an entirely different kind of life. Billy Ray expressed his worries about his daughter in a song he wrote, "Ready, Set, Don't Go." Later, the two would

"READY, SET, DON'T GO" ||||||||||||||||||||||||||||||||||||||||||||||||||||||||

The song "Ready, Set, Don't Go," was written by Billy Ray as Miley prepared to leave for California to take the role of Hannah Montana. It later became a Top 40 hit when Miley and Billy Ray performed it as a duet in 2007. The song expresses Billy Ray's mixed feelings about Miley's success. He was excited for her career to take off, but also felt worried about letting her go.

From left: Mitchel Musso, Billy Ray, Miley, Emily Osment, and Jason Earles were the main actors in *Hannah Montana.*

perform the song together, as a moving duet about a father having a hard time letting go.

But as it turned out, Billy Ray did not have to let go quite yet. When producers offered Miley the role, they had a brilliant idea. Why not have Billy Ray, her real-life dad, play her onscreen father? Billy Ray was uncertain. "The last thing I would want to do is screw up Miley's show," he said.[8] But when he came to an audition with Miley, there was no question it was meant to be. The two laughed, shared inside jokes, and even sang together. The loving relationship between the real-life father and daughter was way more real than anything two actors could portray. Not only was their playful interaction real, it was warm, funny, and entertaining. It worked.

Billy Ray took the part and his character was named Robby Ray Stewart. Miley's character, originally Zoe Stewart, was renamed Miley Stewart. The entire family moved to Los Angeles, and filming began on the show that would make Miley a superstar.

||||||||||||

A SECOND FAMILY ||||||||||||||||||||||||||||||||||||||||||||||||||||||||||||||||||||||||||||||||||||||||||||||||||||

Besides Miley Stewart, the Stewart family included an older brother, Jackson, played by Jason Earles. In the show, Miley and Jackson's mother had passed away, although she appeared on the show in flashbacks, played by actress Brooke Shields.

Miley's character had two best friends, Oliver Oken and Lilly Truscott, played by Mitchel Musso and Emily Osment. The cast was Miley's second family for the five years she worked on the show, and Musso and Osment would become her real-life best friends.

Hannah Montana's plot about a regular girl leading a double life as a celebrity was a hit with young fans.

CHAPTER 5

Hannah Montana

||||||||||||||||||||||||||||||||||||||||||||||||||||

Hannah Montana premiered on March 24, 2006, and immediately became a sensation. Some 5.4 million people watched the first show, giving Disney its highest ratings in the channel's history.[1] Soon, it was the most popular cable show for viewers aged six to 14. *Hannah* was renewed each year for four seasons and was a huge part of Miley's life from ages 12 to 18.

Part of the reason for the show's success was it allowed fans to live out their fantasies of being famous. Miley Stewart seemed like every other ordinary eighth grader struggling with homework, friends, and an annoying brother. But secretly, she was a world-famous pop star, Hannah Montana. Fans wished they could be like Miley, or at least be her friend.

It made sense Miley's character seemed real to viewers. In a way, Miley was playing herself. Just like the real Miley, the Miley on the show was a girl from Tennessee who had moved to California to become a star. She rode horses, sang, and played

A STAR WITH A SECRET

Miley Stewart is a 14-year-old girl who has reached fame as the pop star Hannah Montana but keeps it a secret from friends at school, fearing they won't like her for who she really is. In the first episode, Miley's best friend, Lilly Truscott, surprises Miley with two tickets to the Hannah Montana concert. Miley doesn't want to spill her secret. But she has a dilemma: how can she attend the concert and be onstage at the same time? Lilly learns the truth when she sneaks into Hannah's dressing room. She, along with Oliver Oken, another pal, help keep Miley's secret. They continue to be loyal friends, emphasizing that friends and family matter more than fame.

One running joke on *Hannah Montana* poked fun at Robby Ray's unhealthy diet, especially his love for pie.

the guitar. She also had a former rock star as a father, played by Miley's real-life rock star dad. "From the very beginning, I felt like I *was* Hannah," Miley recalled. "I just felt as though the part was written perfectly for me."[2]

LIFE ON THE SET

Even though she knew she was right for the role, Miley was nervous when filming began.

Her costars, Jason Earles, Emily Osment, and Mitchell Musso, had far more experience than she did. But when she arrived on set, she found everyone was friendly. "On set nobody was judging me," she recalled. "I was working with a team, trying to make the best show we could."[3]

The team quickly became friends. "This group got really tight, really quickly," said costar Jason Earles, who played Miley's brother Jackson.[4] As with all groups of friends, there was jealousy and competition. But for the most part, Miley recalled, "We [were] like a big ol' family, just best friends."[5]

The show was a comedy, with plenty of gags. To keep her identity a secret from everyone, Miley Stewart wears a blonde wig when performing as Hannah Montana. The other characters wear silly disguises as well to help with her ruse. Robby Ray wears a fake mustache, Lilly wears brightly colored wigs, and Oliver dons a fake goatee. Practical jokes were common on the show and on the set. In one episode, Miley smashes a pie in her own face to keep her identity a secret. Several running jokes were aimed at Billy Ray's star past, poking fun at his mullet and the song "Achy Breaky Heart."

MILEY'S FIRST LOVE

Miley's first love was Nick Jonas, a member of the band the Jonas Brothers. They met at a pediatric AIDS fund-raiser in June 2006 and found they had much in common. They were the same age, and both were teen idols who came from Christian families. The night they met, they stayed up until four in the morning talking. "It felt like the whole world stopped. Nothing else mattered. . . . I was so in love," Miley wrote in her autobiography, referring to Nick as "Prince Charming."[6] They got closer when Nick and his family moved to a house in Los Angeles only a few blocks away from Miley. They dated for a year and a half, and although they tried to keep their relationship a secret from fans, "Niley"—the combination of "Nick" and "Miley"—became known as a teen power couple.

Guest stars on the show included Miley's godmother Dolly Parton, who appeared as Miley's aunt on an episode called "Good Golly Miss Dolly" in the first season. During *Hannah*'s second season, an episode titled "Me and Mr. Jonas and Mr. Jonas and Mr. Jonas" featured the popular boy band the Jonas Brothers. Fans did not know it at the time, but Miley was actually dating the youngest member of the group, Nick Jonas. The two had met in June 2006 at an AIDS benefit when Miley was 13.

ROCKING THE SHOW

Acting on the set was only one part of Miley's job. She also had to perform live in concert as Hannah Montana. In the fall of 2006, after filming the first season of the show, 13-year-old Miley went on tour as the opening act for the girl band the Cheetah Girls.

Hannah Montana's music was already familiar to fans of the hit show. The show's theme song, "The Best of Both Worlds," had been popular since it debuted in March. But Miley had no idea if anyone would care to see Hannah Montana in concert. Backstage before the first show, wearing the blonde Hannah wig, she was nervous:

> I felt really little up there on stage. I was really little. Why should I be up there? How could I ever win over that many people?[7]

But when Miley finally relaxed and started singing the first song, "I've Got Nerve," she found the crowd was singing along with her, and they knew every word. Soon she could hear them chanting "Hannah!" and "Miley!" She looked out at a sea of girls in Hannah Montana T-shirts and realized the crowd was there not just for the Cheetah Girls—they were there for her.

Miley performed 20 shows with the Cheetah Girls. On October 24, 2006, Disney released the album *Hannah Montana*, a soundtrack containing all the music from the show. It debuted at Number 1 on the *Billboard* music chart. Hannah Montana was officially a real-life rock star.

|||||||||||||||||||||||||||||||||||||||||||||||||||||

THE WIG |||||||||||||||||||||||||||||||||||||||||||||||||||||||||||||||||||||||||||||||||||||||||||||||||

When in character as Hannah Montana onstage and on the set, Miley had to wear a custom-fitted blonde wig. "If you've never experienced a wig fitting, let me tell you—it's not very glamorous," she wrote in her autobiography.[8] Wearing the Hannah wig at performances was uncomfortable too. The wig could be hot, itchy, and so heavy Miley sometimes worried it would fall off during a concert. When *Hannah* wrapped after four seasons, Miley joked she planned to burn her wig. "I just can't put it on again. It's too much," she said.[9]

Even when she wasn't wearing the wig, Miley's hair on the show wasn't real. Her long brunette locks were created by hundreds of hair extensions. These can take up to three hours to put in, a process costing thousands of dollars every couple of months.

FAME: THE NEW NORMAL

The success of the show meant almost overnight fame for Miley and her costars. Miley felt the change immediately after the first episode aired on television. She described one experience at an amusement park:

> *We were on our way to the roller coaster, when six thirteen-year-old girls ran up to me and asked for my autograph. I did an internal roundoff-back handspring-backflip for joy![10]*

That first encounter was only the beginning. Soon, fans began going crazy. On one occasion, when she was at a mall, so many fans crowded around her the store had to close so she could shop. "Pictures of Miley—of all of us—every time we stepped outside. . . . It became part of normal life," Billy Ray said.[11]

Miley took the attention in stride. Coming out of her house to find as many as 40 photographers waiting didn't bother her. When asked about how well adjusted she seemed, Miley explained, "I don't get shaken or stirred up over anything. . . . I just don't let things faze me. I'm very much like my dad. My dad's like this."[12]

The success of *Hannah Montana* made Miley an overnight sensation with a legion of adoring fans.

As the star of her own hit show and a genuine pop star who performed for crowds of screaming fans, Miley truly had the best of both worlds—acting and singing. She was also able to be a star and keep family by her side. Her father was her costar, and her mom was helping manage her career. Her dreams had come true, but for Miley this was only the beginning.

||||||||||

Miley hoped to reveal more of herself apart from Hannah Montana during her commercially successful Best of Both Worlds Tour across North America.

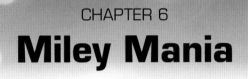

CHAPTER 6
Miley Mania

Hannah Montana had made Miley wildly famous. But most fans knew her onscreen character, not the real Miley. They couldn't tell the difference between Miley Stewart, the character, and Miley Cyrus, the real person. Because Miley's mother on the show had died, rumors spread that Tish was not Miley's real mother. And because Miley performed concerts in character as Hannah Montana, wearing a blonde wig, young

HANNAH VS. MILEY

Although fans often confused Miley Cyrus with her onscreen character, Hannah Montana, Miley emphasized she was very different from the fictional pop star she played. Tomboy Miley hated getting dressed up and preferred wearing sweats and going barefoot to dresses and heels. She included the following list in her autobiography of

"Ways I'm not like Hannah:

1. I'm not perfect.

2. I don't like bright colors.

3. I don't like heels.

4. I don't wear a wig.

5. I'm bad at secrets.

6. I'm not cool.

7. My dad's not really my manager (thank goodness!)"[1]

fans thought Hannah was a real person. When they recognized Miley, they often screamed, "Hannah!"

INTRODUCING MILEY

As the show's popularity continued growing during the second season, Disney felt it was time to introduce Miley as herself. A second soundtrack album, titled *Hannah Montana 2: Meet Miley Cyrus*, was released on June 26, 2007. The album was made up of two discs. The first was the soundtrack to the show's second season, all credited to the fictional star Hannah Montana. But the second album contained music by Miley Cyrus. Miley wrote or contributed to most of the songs herself, and they were more personal and meaningful for her. She explained:

> Hannah has a different message. Hannah's songs are about what it's like to be a famous person when you're an ordinary girl at heart. Her songs . . . are fun to sing, but I am not as emotionally attached to them. . . . My songs are about things that are meaningful to me.[2]

The most personal song on the album was probably "I Miss You," which Miley wrote about her grandfather, Ron Cyrus, who died from lung cancer in 2006. The song "See You Again" became her first Top 10 hit and went platinum. It contains a line referencing her real-life best friend Lesley, who had been her pal since her cheerleading days back in Nashville: "My best friend Lesley said / 'She's just being Miley.'"[3]

‖‖‖

From left: Kevin, Joseph, and Nicholas Jonas of the Jonas Brothers were the opening act for most of the Best of Both Worlds Tour.

A SOLD-OUT TOUR

Fans also loved Miley being Miley. *Hannah Montana 2: Meet Miley Cyrus* immediately soared to Number 1. It would go on to sell at least 4 million copies, making it certified quadruple platinum. Miley was the youngest performer ever to have two Number 1 albums in just 12 months.

In the fall of 2007, Miley began her second concert tour, called the Best of Both Worlds. The Jonas Brothers, Aly & AJ, and Everlife were her opening acts. During each show, Miley performed one set as Hannah Montana and the second half as herself. She toured 59 cities around the United States, playing for audiences of 10,000 to 20,000 people. Tickets sold out in minutes. Although they originally cost between $26 and $66, many of the tickets were resold at many times the price. In their eagerness to see Hannah in concert, fans were willing to pay $200 or even $4,500 for a seat.

After the tour was over, fans across the country packed theaters to see the concert in a 3-D documentary film, *Miley Cyrus: The Best of Both Worlds*. The film was released in February 2008 and earned more than $31 million in just one weekend. Miley Mania had officially taken the nation by storm.

|||||||||||

MERCHANDISE

Hannah Montana was unstoppable. The show appeared in 118 countries, and the soundtrack sold more than 2 million copies.[4] With *Hannah's* popularity, Disney realized it could sell much more than just CDs and DVDs. Beginning in 2007, *Hannah Montana* clothing, jewelry, cosmetics, fragrances, dolls, and toys appeared in stores. Hannah's face appeared on towels, sheets, pens, notebooks, and even lunch boxes.

Even with a successful tour and album, Miley started feeling the pressures of growing up in the spotlight.

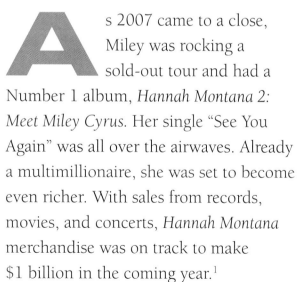

CHAPTER 7

Breaking Out

As 2007 came to a close, Miley was rocking a sold-out tour and had a Number 1 album, *Hannah Montana 2: Meet Miley Cyrus.* Her single "See You Again" was all over the airwaves. Already a multimillionaire, she was set to become even richer. With sales from records, movies, and concerts, *Hannah Montana* merchandise was on track to make $1 billion in the coming year.[1]

Miley was a rich and famous superstar. But she was also 15 years old, and like all teenagers, she was suffering growing pains. Paparazzi waited outside her door. "I didn't believe I was beautiful. Nothing could change that fact," she said.[2]

Miley also experienced her first painful breakup when her relationship with Nick Jonas ended in December 2007. They had shared a genuine love, but the pressures of their overscheduled lives made it difficult to have a relationship. Still, Miley was devastated after the breakup.

Breakout, Miley's third album, debuted on July 22, 2008. Miley wrote eight of the album's 12 songs and said, "I want to be a songwriter for the rest of my life. I love it and it's my escape."[3]

Breakout was Miley's third chart-topping album, and it sold at least 1 million albums to be certified platinum. It received generally good reviews from critics, who felt the album showed promise for Miley to have a lasting career beyond teenage pop idol. One critic noted, "Miley Cyrus does not intend to simply be a TV-generated phenomenon in the pop music world. She is a compelling pop artist in her own right."[4]

Miley's breakup with Nick Jonas served as musical inspiration.

GIVING BACK

Miley noted in her autobiography whenever she felt sorry for herself, charity work helped her keep it all in perspective. She was able to forget her own problems by helping others. She dropped off copies of her third album to a children's hospital and brought smiles to the faces of critically ill children. "I'm the luckiest girl in the world," exclaimed one fan.[5]

Through the Make-a-Wish Foundation, Miley visited many sick children who wished to meet

WRITING HER OWN SONGS

Writing a majority of the songs on *Breakout* provided an outlet for Miley to deal with painful experiences. Critics liked her song "Fly on the Wall," an electro-pop song directed at paparazzi and reporters who try to learn "all my precious secrets."[7] Heartache over her breakup with Nick Jonas fueled a new hit, "7 Things." In the song, a fast-paced pop rock tune, Miley belts out an angry list of "seven things I hate" about a boyfriend, but then the mood shifts and she lists "seven things I like . . . that make me love you."[8] In the video for the song, Miley wears medical tags belonging to Nick, a diabetic. Other girls are shown crying and holding mementoes inspired by real-life gifts from Nick. The video was nominated for an MTV Video Music Award. When it premiered in June 2008, it became one of the most-watched videos on YouTube. Nick also inspired another song on the album, "Full Circle."

their favorite celebrity. "Seeing the children suffering—and surviving—was a jolt," she said.[6]

On September 5, 2008, she recorded the charity song, "Just Stand Up," along with other artists including Beyoncé, Carrie Underwood, and Rihanna. Downloads of the song on iTunes raised money for cancer research. The singers also performed the song during a television special benefitting Stand Up to Cancer, a program encouraging the entertainment industry to help fight cancer. In 2009, during her Wonder World Tour, she donated one dollar from every ticket sold to the City of Hope charity for cancer research.

In November 2008, Miley reached an important milestone when she turned 16. Disney threw her a birthday party in October 2008 at Disneyland in Anaheim, California, which was also a fundraiser. Guests paid $250 to attend and a portion of the proceeds went to Youth Service America, a volunteer organization.

Miley also visited Haiti several times, distributing hearing aids to the needy. In 2010, when a devastating earthquake hit the island nation, Miley joined celebrity artists including Justin Bieber, Nick Jonas, Pink, and Kanye West to record the charity song "We Are the World 25 for Haiti." DoSomething.org has named Miley one of the most charitable celebrities for several years running as of 2014.

||||||||||||||||||||||||||||||||||||||||||||||||||||||

SCANDAL

Miley's growing pains included several scandals in early 2008. Photos of her in underwear and a swimsuit were leaked to the media by a hacker who accessed her email account. Shortly afterward, in April 2008, more photos of Miley caused another uproar. She and her father, Billy Ray, were photographed for *Vanity Fair* magazine by well-known photographer Annie Liebowitz. In one photo, 15-year-old Miley was shown draped only in a sheet with her bare back showing. When the photos went public, many fans complained Miley was too young to be pictured in such a way and it set a bad example to her young fans. A Disney spokesperson condemned the photos, saying *Vanity Fair* had set out to "deliberately manipulate a 15-year-old in order to sell magazines."[9]

Miley apologized for the photos in a statement, saying, "I took part in a photo shoot that was supposed to be 'artistic' and now . . . I feel so embarrassed," she said. Talking about the leaked photos, she added, "The pictures of me on the Internet were silly, inappropriate shots. . . . I am truly sorry if I have disappointed anyone."[10]

Despite the apologies, it was hard not to notice Miley was growing up. In the midst of it all, Miley had her name legally changed from Destiny Hope Cyrus to Miley Ray Cyrus. The "Ray" paid tribute

Miley received her very first MTV Video Music Award nomination for her "7 Things" music video in 2008.

to her grandfather and father. The name change was just one more sign Miley was growing up and asserting who she was.

||||||||||

Hannah Montana: The Movie grossed approximately $155.5 million worldwide.

CHAPTER 8

Climbing New Mountains

||||||||||||||||||||||||||||||||||||||||||||||||||||||||||||||||||||||

I n April 2009, the feature film *Hannah Montana: The Movie* premiered. Leading up to its premiere, the movie's soundtrack was released in March 2009. At the beginning of the movie, Miley is shown fighting over a pair of designer shoes. Fame and success has gone to her head. At the urging of her father, Robby Ray, she goes back to the family farm in Tennessee to spend time with her grandmother, rediscover her country roots, and remember what is truly important in life.

The film's soundtrack contains songs by country acts who appear in the movie, including singer Taylor Swift, country group Rascal Flatts, and Billy Ray Cyrus. Miley performed twelve of the songs, including the lead single, "The Climb." The song is about realizing fame and success are not the point of life. Instead, the lyrics focus on "the climb"—or the experience along the way—and how it gives life meaning.

> **"The simple truth is that being at the top— the most famous or the richest or the most successful—isn't my goal. . . . It's about enjoying the chase. It's about having a dream and seeing it in the distance. It's about working for what you want."[1]**
>
> —*MILEY CYRUS*

The song expressed Miley's feelings at the time. At age 16, she was at the pinnacle of her career. But she was eager to move on to climb other mountains.

MILEY'S WEALTH

In 2008, *Forbes* listed Miley at Number 35 on its Celebrity 100 list, estimating she earned $25 million from June 2007 to June 2008.[3] At 15, Miley was wealthier than in her wildest dreams. However, her mother said most of the money was being invested in an account and Miley would not be able to touch it until she was 18. But Miley continued to be charitable with her considerable wealth and celebrity.

NEW ROLES

During 2008, Miley voice acted in Disney's animated film *Bolt*, which premiered on November 21, 2008. Then she looked around for even more leading roles.

Miley particularly liked the 2002 movie *A Walk to Remember* based on a novel by Nicholas Sparks. It is a romantic movie, but also family friendly. Sparks agreed to adapt one of his existing novels into a film for her. He let Miley name her character Ronnie, after her grandfather Ron Cyrus.

Miley was excited when she read the script for *The Last Song*. Her character, Ronnie, was a rebellious teenage girl, darker and angrier than Hannah. It was an opportunity, Miley said, to

Bolt was a success, and critics praised Miley's performance. The film is about a dog caught up in the fame of being a television star. John Travolta voiced Bolt, while Miley provided the voice of Bolt's owner, a young girl named Penny. Miley also cowrote a song for the film, "I Thought I Lost You." She and Travolta sang it as a duet, and Miley received a Golden Globe nomination for the song.

"actually see if I'm a good actor or not or just good at playing myself."[2]

In the film, Ronnie is sent to spend the summer with her estranged father, a composer. A talented pianist, Ronnie has been offered a scholarship to attend Juilliard, a prestigious music school in New York. Out of anger at her father, she refuses to pursue a career in music. But over the course of the story she forgives her father, falls in love, and finds herself.

||||||||||||||||||||||||||||||||||||||||||||||||||||||||||||||

MILEY IN LOVE

Filming for the movie began in June 2009. It was filmed on Tybee Island, Georgia. When Miley got to know her costar, Australian actor Liam

Miley and Travolta performed a duet of
"I Thought I Lost You" for *Bolt*.

Hemsworth, she fell head over heels. At the time, the handsome actor was unknown in the United States, but he made an impression on Miley. At 19, he was a few years older than Miley and nearly a foot taller. "I got a little nervous about how big he was," she said.[4]

Miley, 16, considered her relationship with Hemsworth to be her first real, adult relationship. Before meeting Hemsworth, she had broken up with country singer and model Justin Gaston after nine months of dating. "The last thing I

While filming, Miley started dating her *Last Song* costar, Liam Hemsworth.

was expecting to do was to fall in love," she said. "But I guess God was like, 'Girl, here is this amazing guy.'"[5]

WONDER WORLD TOUR

But Miley was so busy she hardly had time to savor her new relationship. In August 2009, she released an extended play (EP) called *The Time of Our Lives*. A catchy dance pop tune from the album, "Party in the USA," became her most successful song yet. It debuted at Number 2 on the *Billboard* Hot 100. As she described it, the album "is a transitioning album. . . . really to introduce people to what I want my next record to sound like."[6]

As soon as filming wrapped on *The Last Song*, Miley started rehearsing for her Wonder World Tour. It started in September with 45 concerts in cities all across the United States, England, and Ireland. It would be her first chance to perform with her brother, Trace Cyrus. His band, Metro Station, was her opening act. And perhaps most exciting, it was her first tour as herself.

Miley saw the tour as offering "more of a mature show," aimed at teenagers her age, 16. Although she performed several country-tinged songs from her movie, most of her music was pop rock, a sound she preferred. She closed every show with "The Climb."

||||||||||||

A ROYAL PERFORMANCE ||||||||||||||||||||||||||||||||||||||||||||||||||||||||||||

One of the last stops on Miley's Wonder World Tour was Lancashire, England, where Miley performed for Queen Elizabeth and other members of the royal family at the Royal Variety Performance gala. Although she's not known for being shy, Miley admitted she was very nervous while meeting the queen. Miley also got to meet President Barack Obama and First Lady Michelle Obama when she performed the Kids' Inaugural Concert in January 2009.

Cyrus performed at the
World Wish Day Celebration
in April 2010 to benefit the
Make-A-Wish Foundation.

CHAPTER 9

Untamed

||||||||||||||||||||||||||||||||||||||||||||||||||||||||||||||

As the fourth and final season of *Hannah Montana* began filming in January 2010, Cyrus was less than excited. *Hannah* had made her famous, but now she couldn't wait for it to be over. She felt she'd outgrown the role and the fun was gone. "As I've grown into it, I've grown out of it," she explained to *Parade* magazine.[1]

Billy Ray noted, "She didn't want to do another season. She was done with the wigs and sparkle." He understood

With *Can't Be Tamed*, Cyrus started to show signs she was shedding her wholesome Disney star image.

his daughter's decision. "She wasn't a follower," he said. "From the beginning, she had a sense of wanting to blaze her own trail. . . . To her, *Hannah* was just the start. She was eager to discover what was next."[2]

NOT A DOLL OR A ROBOT

One of the things Cyrus disliked most about her career with Disney was the lack of control she had over her image. A company whose target market was kids, teens, and families, Disney was highly concerned about the image of its stars. Cyrus was a product Disney was selling and she had to fit what the consumers wanted. Everything from her music to her clothing to what she said or did in public was carefully controlled to make sure it fit her wholesome, Disney star image. But Cyrus, now 17, wanted to be her own person. As she told *Parade* magazine in March 2010:

> I hate being thought of as a product. It's my biggest pet peeve. . . . I am not a doll, and people want to treat me that way. They say, 'Now this is what we need to do to your makeup, and this is what I want you to wear,' and I'm like, 'Dude, I choose.' When I was 12, that was okay. But I'm older now. I have an opinion. I have my own taste.[3]

"When I was 12, I thought, 'I want to be famous all the time! I want everybody to recognize me! When they're putting me in sparkles and in pink this final season, I have to grit my teeth. I can't breathe looking like that anymore. . . . I'm feeling claustrophobic in all these frills."[4]

—MILEY CYRUS

Cyrus's rebellious attitude continued attracting negative attention. In August 2009, she was criticized for her performance at the Teen Choice Awards, which involved dancing on a pole atop an ice cream cart. Some compared it to a stripper's pole. A video taken by friends in November 2010 at a party to celebrate her eighteenth birthday leaked in December. It showed Cyrus smoking what appeared to be marijuana. She later said it was actually salvia, an herb legal in the state of California. Still, she apologized for the incident, realizing she had failed as a role model for her young fans. "I'm not perfect," Cyrus said. "I made a mistake. . . . I'm disappointed in myself for disappointing my fans."[6]

Cyrus's father, Billy Ray, also apologized to fans for the incident. "I'm so sad. There is much beyond my control right now," he wrote in a statement.[7] In a March 2011 interview for GQ magazine, he admitted he was scared for Cyrus and said, "As her daddy I'd like to try to help. Take care of her just a little bit."[8] But Cyrus was 18, and she was going to do what she wanted.

Cyrus also expressed her frustration in several songs on her album *Can't Be Tamed*, released in June 2010. The song "Robot" includes the lyrics "I'm not your robot / Stop telling me I'm part of the big machine."[5] In the music video for the title song, "Can't Be Tamed," she is shown as a large exotic bird in a cage, being gawked at by a curious crowd. The audience recoils in fear as she spreads out her huge black wings and breaks free from the cage.

‖‖‖

"I've gone these past five years with everyone telling me what to do. Now it's up to me and what I think is right for my career, so I'm just going in my own direction. . . . I love making movies. That's what I want to pursue. It's not that I don't love music. . . . If every film could have music in [it], I would do that. But I feel that I need to get away from that for a little while. It's my security blanket and I don't always want to fall back on that."[9]

—*MILEY CYRUS*

REBEL ROCKER

There were no Hannah-style sequins and sparkles on the album cover for *Can't Be Tamed*. Instead, Cyrus is pictured in midriff-baring black leather with a defiant pout. The pose on the cover was inspired by one of her heroes, rebel rocker Joan Jett, whose songs "Bad Reputation" and "I Love Rock and Roll" were hits in the 1980s. When Cyrus got a chance to meet her idol in 2011, she told Jett: "I have always looked up [to] you. When you came out people were shocked that there was a chick that wanted to rock as hard as the guys."[10]

Cyrus kept the black leather look throughout her Gypsy Heart Tour, when she toured Australia, Latin America, and the Philippines starting in April 2011. Although her look was edgy, her own songs on *Can't Be Tamed* were still mainly dance pop in style, not hard rock. But it was a step toward the adult image she wanted. To critics who said she was betraying her young fans who loved her as Hannah, she said, "I'm not stepping away from my younger fans, I'm maturing."[11]

||||||||||||||||||||||||||||||||||||||||||||||||||||||||||||

MOVING IN HER OWN DIRECTION

Can't Be Tamed was Cyrus's final recording with Hollywood Records, which was owned by Disney. When it was finished, she announced she was taking a break from her music career to focus on acting.

Cyrus hoped *The Last Song* would lead to a career in acting. But when the reviews came

The Last Song was a commercial success but critical failure.

out after its release on March 31, 2010, she was crushed. Although the film did well in theaters, critics slammed it. Many criticized the script as being too sentimental and unrealistic, but they also

Cyrus performed her song "Forgiveness and Love" at the 2010 American Music Awards.

blamed Cyrus's performance. Although she had been successful as the star of a television comedy, critics felt Cyrus did not have the acting talent to carry the lead role in a movie. One review in the *New York Times* wrote, "She seems to be mugging for the camera, play-acting rather than exploring the motives and feelings of her character."[12]

Cyrus admitted she probably needed acting lessons. After *Hannah Montana* ended on January 16, 2011, she continued in a few acting roles. She appeared on the MTV series *Punk'd* and a few episodes of the popular sitcom *Two and a Half Men*. But her two films released in 2012, *LOL* and *So Undercover*, were ignored.

In the end, Cyrus admitted her talent and her heart were really in performing, not acting. "I'm gonna do music for the rest of my life," she said.[13]

By 2011, Cyrus had recorded eight top-selling albums. But she wanted to start fresh. "Right now, when people go to iTunes and listen to my old music, it's so irritating to me because I can't just erase that stuff and start over," Cyrus told *Billboard*. "My last record I feel so disconnected from—I was sixteen or seventeen when I made it. When you're in your 20s, you just don't really know that person anymore. . . . I want to start over as a new artist."[14]

||||||||||

Cyrus showed off a new haircut
on the red carpet of the
2012 MTV Video Music Awards.

CHAPTER 10

"Wrecking Ball"

Cyrus continued shaking up her image—including cutting off most of her hair and sporting a new punk-rock buzz cut in August 2012. People who followed her career for the next two years might say she didn't just erase her old image—she took a wrecking ball to it.

Once her contract with Hollywood Records ended, she signed with RCA Records and found a new manager, Larry Rudolph. Rudolph previously managed singer Britney Spears, who had similarly transitioned from teen idol to serious performer. But before she could make a new album, Cyrus had to find herself.

"I didn't know necessarily what my sound was gonna be," Cyrus recalled in the MTV documentary *Miley: The Movement.* "I needed to know who I was as an artist. Everyone had their idea of what they thought I should be doing, who I should be working with."[1]

In 2012, Cyrus explored different musical styles. She recorded covers of classic songs by a variety of artists, including Dolly Parton, Nirvana, and Bob Dylan. The sessions showcased the power of Cyrus's naturally husky voice and proved she could sing almost any kind of song. Now she had to choose which genres fit her best.

With her Nashville roots and Tennessee twang, many predicted Cyrus would find success as a country singer. But Cyrus liked all kinds of music. As a child, she'd heard Elvis Presley, Joan Jett, and Etta James on her father's jukebox. In her teen years she'd loved rock. Now, at age 20, she listened

Producer Mike WiLL helped Cyrus come up with a new sound for *Bangerz*.

to a lot of hip-hop. Hip-hop and rap would be strongly featured on her next album, *Bangerz*.

BANGERZ

Cyrus's sound came together after she connected with artist and producer Mike Williams, known as Mike WiLL. "I got in the studio and we were just in the room bouncing off these ideas, just kinda like singing with each other," she said.[2] Cyrus

Of all the artists she worked with while recording *Bangerz*, Cyrus was most excited about doing a song with Britney Spears. Spears's voice is featured on "Bangerz," the album's title track. Cyrus had idolized Spears ever since she was a girl. The first record she ever bought was Spears's 1999 album, . . . *Baby One More Time*. "I'll be a diehard fan for Britney, always," she said.[3]

also worked with producers Dr. Luke and Pharrell Williams. The result was a hip-hop flavored pop album featuring rappers Juicy J, French Montana, and Big Sean, as well as Nelly, Future, Will.I.am, and Britney Spears.

The mix worked. Cyrus's first single, the party song "We Can't Stop," was released on June 3, 2013. It soared to Number 2 on *Billboard's* Hot 100 and was Number 1 on iTunes as its most downloaded song. The breakup ballad "Wrecking Ball" was Cyrus's second single from the album. Released right after her controversial performance at the 2013 VMAs, it quickly soared to Number 1 on the *Billboard* Hot 100.

Bangerz was released in October 2013 and sold 270,000 copies in the first week. It reached

Number 1 on the *Billboard* charts and quickly went platinum. Critics praised it, too. *Billboard* magazine called it "fiercely individual."[4] *Entertainment Weekly* said it was "utterly fresh."[5] The album was named one of the best of 2013 by *Rolling Stone* magazine. Journalist Barbara Walters listed Cyrus one of the Most Fascinating People of 2013.

A CONTROVERSIAL IMAGE

Cyrus wanted everything about her image to be new. "Everything has to feel new and creative and pushing the boundaries," she said.[6] Cyrus's new sound was different. Her new hairstyle also made a statement about how she was changing as an artist. One commentator said, "It was the kind of haircut

AN EXPENSIVE LIFESTYLE

Following the success of *Bangerz*, Cyrus was richer than ever before. *Parade* magazine estimated she had earned $76.5 million in 2013. Her lifestyle reflected her growing wealth. At the beginning of her career, Cyrus wore clothing from Forever 21 and Target.

Today, her closet is bursting with expensive designer outfits. Chanel, Marc Jacobs, and Versace are her favorites. One gown she wore to a gala in 2013 cost $9,000, and a Cartier bracelet she owns cost $36,000.

Cyrus performed on the *Today Show* to promote *Bangerz* on October 7, 2013.

that let everyone know: 'You're not going to see the old Miley again, so say goodbye and buckle your seatbelts for the new one.'"[7]

The new haircut was tame compared to the way Cyrus dressed and acted. In her music videos, Cyrus wore tiny, tight outfits revealing multiple tattoos on her body. The video for "Wrecking Ball" even showed her naked. She became known for sticking her tongue out in photographs and twerking. To many critics, Cyrus seemed to be determined to behave in the raunchiest manner possible.

Perhaps the most controversial issue was Cyrus's association with drugs. The lyrics to the song "We

Can't Stop" hinted at drug use, and Cyrus was photographed smoking marijuana while in concert in Amsterdam, where smokers can't be prosecuted for possession of small amounts. Cyrus said she was making a joke, but parents and experts were not laughing. In May 2014, when Cyrus was hospitalized for a reaction to antibiotics, rumors spread that it was a drug overdose. Cyrus denied she had overdosed, saying, "I am the poster child for good health."[8]

GOING IT ALONE

In September 2013, shortly after her performance at the VMAs, Cyrus announced she had broken up with Liam Hemsworth. Hemsworth and Cyrus had been on-again, off-again for four years, and even got engaged in June 2012, when Cyrus was 19.

NOT A RAPPER

Even though many rappers are featured on her album, Cyrus emphasized she was still a pop singer, not a rapper or hip-hop artist. "My talent is as a singer," she said. "I've always wanted country-rock influences, but now I'm moving over to a more urban side. It's not a hip-hop album, though—it's a pop album. I'm not coming in trying to rap."[9]

One of the reasons for the breakup was she was too young. She had wanted to break up for some time, but was afraid. "I was so scared of ever being alone," she said. "I think conquering that fear, this year, was actually bigger than any other transition I had, this entire year."[10]

After watching Cyrus's video of her breakup song "Wrecking Ball," many fans wonder if the song was about Hemsworth. Cyrus did not write the song, but her tearful performance in the video may in fact have been directed toward him. Cyrus admitted to talk show host Ellen DeGeneres many of the songs on her album were about her relationship. Looking back, she said, "I think I knew more intuitively where my life was going than I actually thought I did at the time."[11]

Following her breakup, Cyrus wasn't totally alone. She purchased a mansion only a few doors down from her family home in Toluca Lake, California. Billy Ray often stopped by to visit. He was supportive of her career moves, even recording a hip-hop version of "Achy Breaky Heart." Tish remained her comanager and was by her side during the making of her album.

As always, Cyrus credited the support of her family with helping her stay grounded.

||||||||||||||||||||||||||||||||||||||||||||||||||||||||||||||

JUST BEING MILEY

Cyrus launched her Bangerz Tour in February 2014. Like her album, it was full of zany surprises, such as a giant inflatable balloon of her dog Floyd and dancers in furry animal costumes. Cyrus entered the stage by sliding down a giant pink tongue and left on an enormous flying hot dog. And during the show, Cyrus said she wasn't going to be afraid of making fun of herself. "That's what I think I've been representing, more than anything, in the past year," she said. "Being fun and carefree, and that's really what the show represents."[12]

SONGS FITTING HER LIFE ||||||||||||||||||||||||||||||||||||||||||||||||||||||||

Even though Cyrus did not write all of the songs on *Bangerz*, her song choices and her performances reflect her life at the time. "We Can't Stop," a song about a wild house party, was written by Mike WiLL with Rihanna in mind, but Cyrus felt it fit her life. "I'm 20 years old and I want to talk to the people that are up all night with their friends."[13] As for the video, she said, "It's based on a true story of a crazy night I had. When I heard the song for the first time, it captured exactly what I was living."[14]

To those who criticized Cyrus's new image, she said, "I feel like the best way of fighting my haters is just keep . . . doing what you do. Success is the best form of revenge."[15] She counted on her many fans, called Smilers, for support.

In August 2014, Cyrus won Video of the Year for "Wrecking Ball," the top honor at the 2014 MTV VMAs. Cyrus's date, Jesse Helt, accepted the award on her behalf. Helt was homeless as a teenager and met Cyrus at My Friend's Place, a homeless youth center in Los Angeles. He used his speech to raise awareness about the issue of homelessness in the United States.

After the success of *Bangerz*, Cyrus said she had reached the point in her career where she can be who she wants. She said,

> *It's not like I'm losing who I am—I actually found out more about who I am by making this music. I'm going on a journey . . . And I'm still going to change so much. Because I'm not the same person I was six months ago—I'm not even the same person I was two weeks ago.*[16]

Love her or hate her, whoever Cyrus is today, it's sure to change. And the world will be watching.

‖‖‖‖‖‖

At the 2014 VMAs, Helt accepted Cyrus's award for Video of the Year, using the platform to raise awareness about homeless youth.

TIMELINE

1992

Destiny Hope Cyrus, nicknamed "Miley," is born on November 23.

2001-2003

Cyrus appears on three episodes of the television series *Doc*.

2003

Cyrus plays a small role in the film *Big Fish*.

2007

The soundtrack album *Hannah Montana 2: Meet Miley Cyrus* is released on June 26.

2007

Cyrus's sold-out Best of Both Worlds concert tour begins in the fall.

2008

Hannah Montana & Miley Cyrus: Best of Both Worlds Concert, a 3-D film of Cyrus's concert tour, packs theaters in February.

2004

2006

2006

At age 12, Cyrus is chosen to star in the Disney Channel series *Hannah Montana.*

Hannah Montana premieres on March 24 with Cyrus in the lead role.

The *Hannah Montana* soundtrack album is released on October 24; "Best of Both Worlds" appears on the *Billboard* Hot 100.

2008

2008

2009

Cyrus's album *Breakout* is released July 22.

Cyrus's animated film *Bolt* premieres on November 21.

On March 12, Cyrus releases "The Climb," a song from the *Hannah Montana: The Movie* soundtrack.

TIMELINE

2009

Hannah Montana: The Movie premieres on April 10.

2009

In August, "Party in the USA" debuts at Number 2 on *Billboard*'s Hot 100.

2009

Cyrus starts the Wonder World Tour in September.

2011

Cyrus performs on her Gypsy Heart Tour from April to July.

2013

"We Can't Stop," the first single from Cyrus's new album, *Bangerz*, debuts on June 3.

2013

Cyrus gives a controversial performance at the MTV Video Music Awards on August 25.

2010

2010

2011

Cyrus's film *The Last Song* hits theaters on March 31.

Can't Be Tamed is released on June 21.

The *Hannah Montana* finale airs on January 16.

2013

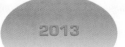

2013

2014

"Wrecking Ball" reaches Number 1 on *Billboard*'s Hot 100.

Bangerz debuts in October and reaches Number 1 on the *Billboard* 200.

"Wrecking Ball" wins Video of the Year at the Video Music Awards.

GET THE SCOOP

FULL NAME

Miley Ray Cyrus (born Destiny Hope Cyrus)

DATE OF BIRTH

November 23, 1992

PLACE OF BIRTH

Franklin, Tennessee

SELECTED ALBUMS

Hannah Montana (2006), *Hannah Montana 2: Meet Miley Cyrus* (2007), *Breakout* (2008), *Can't Be Tamed* (2010), *Bangerz* (2013)

TOURS

Best of Both Worlds Tour (2007), Wonder World Tour (2009), Gypsy Heart Tour (2011), Bangerz Tour (2014)

SELECTED TELEVISION APPEARANCES

Hannah Montana (2006–2011)

SELECTED FILM APPEARANCES

Hannah Montana: The Movie (2009), *The Last Song* (2010), *LOL* (2012), *So Undercover* (2012)

SELECTED AWARDS

- Nominated for 2009 Golden Globe for Best Original Song for "I Thought I'd Lost You" from *Bolt* (2008)
- Won the 2008 MTV Movie Award for Best Song From A Movie for "The Climb"
- Won the 2014 Video Music Award for Video of the Year for "Wrecking Ball"

PHILANTHROPY

Miley Cyrus is an animal lover who supports animal rescue organizations. Through the Make-A-Wish Foundation, she has fulfilled the dreams of many young fans suffering from illnesses. Some of the profits from her Wonder World Tour went to the City of Hope charity for cancer research. She has also supported Youth Service America, Stand Up to Cancer, and victims of the 2010 earthquake in Haiti.

"It's not like I'm losing who I am—I actually found out more about who I am by making this music. I'm going on a journey . . . And I'm still going to change so much. Because I'm not the same person I was six months ago—I'm not even the same person I was two weeks ago."

—*MILEY CYRUS*

GLOSSARY

appropriation—Adopting specific elements of another cultural group, often in an exploitative manner.

audition—A trial hearing given to a singer, actor, or other performer to test suitability for a role, professional training, or competition.

Billboard—A music chart system used by the music recording industry to measure record popularity and sales.

debut—A first appearance.

extended play (EP)—A musical release with more than one song or track, but not enough for an album.

genre—A category of art, music, or literature characterized by a particular style, form, or content.

hip-hop—A style of popular music associated with US urban culture that features rap spoken against a background of electronic music or beats.

idol—A person someone looks up to and admires greatly.

platinum—A certification by the Recording Industry Association of America that an album has sold more than 1 million copies.

pop—A commercial or popular style of music.

producer—Someone who oversees or provides money for a play, television show, movie, or album.

rap—A style of popular music noted for rhythmic speaking of rhymed couplets set to a strong beat.

record label—A brand or trademark related to the marketing of music video and recordings.

single—An individual song that is distributed on its own over the radio and other mediums.

ADDITIONAL RESOURCES

SELECTED BIBLIOGRAPHY

Diehl, Matt. "Miley Cyrus 2.0: The Billboard Cover Story." *Billboard*. Billboard, 14 June 2013. Web. 15 July 2014.

Janic, Susan. *Living the Dream: Hannah Montana and Miley Cyrus, the Unofficial Story*. Toronto: ECW, 2008.

Miley: The Movement. Dir. Paul Bozymowski. MTV, 2013. *MTV*. Viacom, 15 July 2014. Web. 11 Aug. 2014.

FURTHER READINGS

Cyrus, Billy Ray. *Hillbilly Heart*. New York: Houghton Mifflin, 2013. Print.

Cyrus, Miley, and Hilary Liftin. *Miles to Go*. New York: Disney/Hyperion, 2011. Print.

Hester, Beth Landis. *Hannah Montana: The Essential Guide*. New York: DK, 2009. Print.

WEBSITES

To learn more about Contemporary Lives, visit **booklinks.abdopublishing.com**. These links are routinely monitored and updated to provide the most current information available.

PLACES TO VISIT

Disneyland Resort
1313 Disneyland Drive
Anaheim, CA 92802
714-781-4565
https://disneyland.disney.go.com
Explore the amusement park where Cyrus held her 16th
birthday celebration in November 2008. The park, which
opened in 1955, is home to rides and attractions such as the
Haunted Mansion and the iconic Sleeping Beauty's Castle.

Visit Nashville
150 Fourth Avenue North
Nashville, TN 37219
800-657-6910
http://www.visitmusiccity.com
Visit Cyrus's hometown of Nashville, Tennessee, known
as "Music City." Nashville is home to many attractions,
including the Country Music Hall of Fame and Museum.
Music Row, an area southwest of downtown Nashville, is
where many artists, including Elvis, Dolly Parton, and Roy
Orbison, recorded classic songs.

SOURCE NOTES

CHAPTER 1. A SHOCKING PERFORMANCE

1. Rick Kissell. "VMA Awards Bounce Back in the Ratings With 10.1 Million Viewers." *Variety*. Variety Media, 26 Aug. 2013. Web. 15 July 2014.

2. Phillip Mlynar. "Miley Cyrus Twerks, Gives Robin Thicke Some Tongue at VMAs." *MTV*. Viacom, 25 Aug. 2013. Web. 6 Aug. 2014.

3. "We Can't Stop/Blurred Lines/Give It 2 U (Medley)." *MTV*. Viacom, 4 Sept. 2013. Web. 6 Aug. 2014.

4. Ibid.

5. Josh Eells. "Miley Cyrus on Why She Loves Weed, Went Wild at the VMAs and Much More." *Rolling Stone*. Rolling Stone, 7 Sept. 2013. Web. 6 Aug. 2014.

6. Jody Rosen. "Rosen: The 2013 VMAs Were Dominated by Miley's Minstrel Show." *Vulture*. New York Media, 26 Aug. 2013. Web. 6 Aug. 2014.

7. B. J. Steiner. "The Most Awkward Hip-Hop Moments at MTV's 2013 Video Music Awards." *XXL*. Harris Publications, 26 Aug. 2013. Web. 6 Aug. 2014.

8. Kelly Wallace. "Would You Take Kids to See Miley?" *CNN*. CNN, 25 Feb. 2014. Web. 6 Aug. 2014.

9. *Miley: The Movement*. Dir. Paul Bozymowski. MTV, 2013. *MTV*. Viacom, 15 July 2014. Web. 11 Aug. 2014.

10. Zack O'Malley Greenburg. "Miley Cyrus Biggest Winner at VMAs Despite Lack of Awards." *Forbes*. Forbes, 27 Aug. 2013. Web. 11 Aug. 2014.

11. *Miley: The Movement*. Dir. Paul Bozymowski. MTV, 2013. *MTV*. Viacom, 15 July 2014. Web. 11 Aug. 2014.

CHAPTER 2. DAUGHTER OF A COUNTRY STAR

1. Miley Cyrus and Hilary Liftin. *Miles to Go*. New York: Disney/Hyperion, 2009. Print. 79.

2. Ibid. 153.

3. Jackie Robb. *Miley Mania! Behind the Scenes with Miley Cyrus*. New York: Scholastic, 2008. Print. 10.

4. Miley Cyrus and Hilary Liftin. *Miles to Go*. New York: Disney/Hyperion, 2009. Print. 117.

5. Ibid. 130.

6. Ibid. 125.

7. Billy Ray Cyrus. *Hillbilly Heart*. New York: Houghton Mifflin, 2013. Print. 195.

8. Susan Janic. *Living the Dream: Hannah Montana and Miley Cyrus, the Unofficial Story*. Toronto: ECW Press, 2008. Print. 8.

9. Rebecca Macatee. "Dolly Parton Defends Goddaughter Miley Cyrus: She's Just Trying to Find Her Own Place." *E! Online*. E! Online, 4 Nov. 2013. Web. 15 Aug. 2014.

CHAPTER 3. "THIS IS WHAT I WANT TO DO"

1. Miley Cyrus and Hilary Liftin. *Miles to Go*. New York: Disney/Hyperion, 2009. Print. 153–154.

2. *Miley: The Movement*. Dir. Paul Bozymowski. MTV, 2013. *MTV*. Viacom, 15 July 2014. Web. 11 Aug. 2014.

3. Miley Cyrus and Hilary Liftin. *Miles to Go*. New York: Disney/Hyperion, 2009. Print. 24.

4. Ibid.

5. Ibid. 139.

6. Richard Ouzounian. "Miley Cyrus: Teen of All Media." *Thestar.com*. Toronto Star, 4 Apr. 2009. Web. 15 July 2014.

CHAPTER 4. TOUGH ENOUGH TO MAKE IT

1. Miley Cyrus and Hilary Liftin. *Miles to Go*. New York: Disney/Hyperion, 2009. Print. 146.

2. Jackie Robb. *Miley Mania! Behind the Scenes with Miley Cyrus*. New York: Scholastic, 2008. Print. 12.

3. Miley Cyrus and Hilary Liftin. *Miles to Go*. New York: Disney/Hyperion, 2009. Print. 27.

4. Ibid. 53–54.

5. Susan Janic. *Living the Dream: Hannah Montana and Miley Cyrus, the Unofficial Story*. Toronto: ECW Press, 2008. Print. 18.

6. Ibid. 20–21.

7. Ibid.

8. Jacques Steinberg. "A Tale of Two Tweens: One Real and One Disney." *New York Times*. New York Times, 19 Apr. 2006. Web. 15 July 2014.

CHAPTER 5. *HANNAH MONTANA*

1. Ann Oldenburg. "Miley Cyrus Fulfills Her Destiny." *USA Today*. USA Today, 14 Jan. 2007. Web. 15 July 2014.

2. Miley Cyrus and Hilary Liftin. *Miles to Go*. New York: Disney/Hyperion, 2009. Print. 95.

3. Ibid. 93.

4. Lauren Alexander. *Mad for Miley: An Unauthorized Biography*. New York: Price Stern Sloan, 2007. Print. 57.

5. "Meet The Real Miley Cyrus DVD." *YouTube*. YouTube, 6 Aug. 2007. Web. 15 July 2014.

6. Miley Cyrus and Hilary Liftin. *Miles to Go*. New York: Disney/Hyperion, 2009. Print. 150–151.

7. Ibid. 101–102.

8. Ibid. 73.

9. Lauren Franklin. "Miley Cyrus to Leave Music Behind to Concentrate on Acting." *Sugarscape*. Hearst Magazines UK, 16 Mar. 2010. Web. 15 July 2014.

10. Miley Cyrus and Hilary Liftin. *Miles to Go*. New York: Disney/Hyperion, 2009. Print. 74.

11. Billy Ray Cyrus. *Hillbilly Heart*. New York: Houghton Mifflin, 2013. Print. 240.

12. Bruce Handy. "Miley Knows Best." *Vanity Fair*. Condé Nast, June 2008. Web. 15 July 2014.

CHAPTER 6. MILEY MANIA

1. Miley Cyrus and Hilary Liftin. *Miles to Go*. New York: Disney/Hyperion, 2009. Print. 210.

2. Ibid. 183–184.

3. "Miley Cyrus - See You Again Lyrics." *MetroLyrics*. CBS Interactive, n.d. Web. 11 Aug. 2014.

4. Ann Oldenburg. "Miley Cyrus Fulfills Her Destiny." *USA Today*. USA Today, 14 Jan. 2007. Web. 15 July 2014.

CHAPTER 7. BREAKING OUT

1. Gil Kaufman. "Miley Cyrus Is Top Teen Earner." *MTV News*. Viacom, 24 Mar. 2008. Web. 15 July 2014.

2. Miley Cyrus and Hilary Liftin. *Miles to Go*. New York: Disney/Hyperion, 2009. Print. 165.

3. Cortney Harding. "Exclusive: Miley Cyrus Grows Up on 'Breakout.'" *Billboard*. Billboard, 27 June 2008. Web. 11 Aug. 2014.

4. Bill Lamb. "Miley Cyrus—'7 Things.'" *About.com*. About.com, n.d. Web. 15 July 2014.

5. Miley Cyrus and Hilary Liftin. *Miles to Go*. New York: Disney/Hyperion, 2009. Print. 173.

6. Ibid.174–175.

7. "Fly On The Wall Lyrics." *MetroLyrics*. CBS Interactive, n.d. Web. 15 July 2014.

8. "7 Things Lyrics." *MetroLyrics*. CBS Interactive, n.d. Web. 15 July 2014.

9. Stephen M. Silverman. "Miley Cyrus: I'm Sorry for Photos." *People*. Time, 27 Apr. 2008. Web. 11 Aug. 2014.

10. Ibid.

CHAPTER 8. CLIMBING NEW MOUNTAINS

1. Miley Cyrus and Hilary Liftin. *Miles to Go*. New York: Disney/Hyperion, 2009. Print. 125, 214.

2. "10 Qs With 'Hannah Montana' Star Miley Cyrus." *Hollywood.com*. Hollywood.com, n.d. Web. 15 July 2014.

3. "The Celebrity 100." *Forbes*. Forbes, 11 June 2008. Web. 15 July 2014.

4. "Liam Hemsworth Made Miley Cyrus Nervous!" *BOP and Tiger Beat*. BOP and Tiger Beat, 17 Mar. 2010. Web. 15 July 2014.

5. "Life in Photos: Miley Cyrus." *MSN Entertainment*. MSN, n.d. Web. 15 July 2014.

6. "Miley Cyrus Talks Tour, Growing Up, and Twitter Feedback." *Cleveland.com*. Plain Dealer Publishing, 24 Sept. 2009. Web. 15 July 2014.

CHAPTER 9. UNTAMED

1. Kevin Sessums. "Miley Cyrus: 'I Know Who I Am Now.'" *Parade*. Parade, 21 Mar. 2010. Web. 15 July 2014.

2. Billy Ray Cyrus. *Hillbilly Heart*. New York: Houghton Mifflin, 2013. Print. 248.

3. Kevin Sessums. "Miley Cyrus: 'I Know Who I Am Now.'" *Parade*. Parade, 21 Mar. 2010. Web. 15 July 2014.

4. Ibid.

5. "Miley Cyrus Lyrics: 'Robot.'" *AZLyrics.com*. AZLyrics.com, n.d. Web. 11 Aug. 2014.

6. Kimberly Cutter. "The Life of Miley Cyrus." *Marie Claire*. Hearst Communications, 21 July 2011. Web. 15 July 2014.

7. "'I'm So Sad,' Says Billy Ray Cyrus after His Daughter Miley Is Caught Smoking a Bong." *Daily Mail*. Daily Mail, 11 Dec. 2010. Web. 15 July 2014.

8. Chris Heath. "Mr. Hannah Montana's Achy Broken Heart." *GQ*. Condé Nast, Mar. 2011. Web. 15 July 2014.

9. Lauren Franklin. "Miley Cyrus to Leave Music Behind to Concentrate on Acting." *Sugarscape*. Hearst Magazines UK, 16 Mar. 2010. Web. 15 July 2014.

10. Liz Raftery. "Miley Cyrus Thanks Joan Jett for Never Apologizing." *People*. People, 6 Sept. 2011. Web. 15 July 2014.

11. Kate Lucey. "Miley Cyrus: "I'm Not Stepping Away From My Younger Fans, I'm Maturing." *Sugarscape*. Hearst Magazines UK, 10 Oct. 2012. Web. 15 July 2014.

12. A. O. Scott. "Summer Love, a Sea of Trouble." *New York Times*. New York Times, 30 Mar. 2010. Web. 15 July 2014.

13. "Miley Cyrus: 'I'm Gonna Do Music for the Rest of My Life.'" *Celebrity-Gossip.net*. Bluefin Media, 3 Oct. 2013. Web. 11 Aug. 2014.

14. Matt Diehl. "Miley Cyrus 2.0: The Billboard Cover Story." *Billboard*. Billboard, 14 June 2013. Web. 15 July 2014.

CHAPTER 10. "WRECKING BALL"

1. *Miley: The Movement*. Dir. Paul Bozymowski. MTV, 2013. *MTV*. Viacom, 15 July 2014. Web. 11 Aug. 2014.

2. Rebecka Schumann. "Miley Cyrus Talks Mike WiLL." *International Business Times*. IBT Media, 3 Oct. 2013. Web. 11 Aug. 2014.

3. Shamecca Harris. "Britney Spears on Miley Cyrus: 'I Think She's Brilliant.'" *ABC News*. ABC News, 16 Oct. 2013. Web. 15 Jan. 2014.

4. Jason Lipshutz. "Miley Cyrus, 'Bangerz': Track-By-Track Review." *Billboard*. Billboard, 1 Oct. 2013. Web. 15 July 2014.

5. Nick Catucci. "Bangerz Album Review." *Entertainment Weekly*. Entertainment Weekly, 9 Oct. 2013. Web. 15 July 2014.

6. *Miley: The Movement*. Dir. Paul Bozymowski. MTV, 2013. *MTV*. Viacom, 15 July 2014. Web. 11 Aug. 2014.

7. "The Fabulous Life of 'Miley Cyrus.'" *YouTube*. YouTube, 21 June 2014. Web. 15 July 2014.

8. Bonnie Fuller. "Miley Cyrus: Stop Promoting Drugs." *Hollywood Life*. PMC, 17 Mar. 2014. Web. 15 July 2014.

9. Margaret Egby. "Miley Cyrus: People Wanted 'to Make Me the White Nicki Minaj.'" *Daily News*. New York Daily News, 14 June 2014. Web. 15 July 2014.

10. Lauren Effron. "Miley Cyrus Talks Ending Relationship with Liam Hemsworth, Fears Being Alone." *ABC News*. ABC News, 16 Dec. 2013. Web. 15 Jan. 2014.

11. Zach Johnson. "Miley Cyrus Breaks Her Silence on Liam Hemsworth Split: I'm Obsessed With Being Alone." *E! Online*. E! Online, 11 Oct. 2013. Web. 15 July 2014.

12. Ashley Lee. "Miley Cyrus' 'Bangerz' Tour: 8 Things to Expect." *Hollywood Reporter*. Hollywood Reporter, 15 Jan. 2014. Web. 15 July 2014.

13. Carl Smith. "Miley Cyrus on Her New Album: 'I Want to Start as a New Artist.'" *Sugarscape*. Hearst Magazines UK, 16 June 2013. Web. 15 July 2014.

14. Ibid.

15. Rume Ugen. "Miley Cyrus Says Meeting Queen Elizabeth Was the 'Scariest' Moment of Her Life." *EntertainmentWise*. EntertainmentWise, 22 Sept. 2013. Web. 15 July 2014.

16. Matt Diehl. "Miley Cyrus 2.0: The Billboard Cover Story." *Billboard*. Billboard, 14 June 2013. Web. 15 July 2014.

INDEX

ABOUT THE AUTHOR

Jennifer Joline Anderson has been writing since she was a teenager, when she won a contest and had her first short story published in *Seventeen* magazine. She lives with her husband and children, Alex, Ruby, and Henry, in Minneapolis, Minnesota, where she writes educational books for young people.